The People Friendly Introvert

Develop People Skills, Communicate Effectively, Amplify Your Introvert Power, and Thrive In This Extrovert World (Without Sacrificing Your Inner Quiet)

Thomas Lee Watson
thomasleewatsonbooks@gmail.com

Table of Contents

Introduction

Let me tell you about my friend John, who is a successful California-based businessman. He has this uncanny ability to turn trends into a lot of cash.

It's as if he's able to look around the corner as far as consumer tastes go and get in on the ground floor of a lot of business opportunities.

As you can well imagine, this is an awesome skill to have.

The problem with John, if you want to call it a problem, is that he is an introvert in the business world.

If you've ever done any kind of business, you know that, to be successful, you have to know how to reach out. You have to know how to play to the crowd, and you have to read people.

While introverts can do this, my friend John was an extreme introvert.

As you probably already know, introverts are not necessarily shy people. People are shy because they have developed some sort of negative association between public contact or face to face interaction with a lot of people, with some trauma.

That was not the case with John. The problem John had was that social interaction really tires him out very quickly.

So, just like a lot of introverts, he managed to get as far as he could with "faking it until you make it." Basically, he would try to come off as an extrovert, knowing deep down inside that he's an introvert.

To a certain extent, this worked. But when it comes to the really big victories in his life, he told me that he needed to get out from under this lie. It was just sucking him dry.

He would go to meetings and he would meet a lot of people, speak to large crowds of strangers, and he would feel so emotionally spent after all of that that he said he was just shell-shocked.

Even if he wanted to talk to anybody, the words couldn't come out of his mouth. He was just an empty shell. That's how much social interaction drained him.

That's the big difference between introverts and shy people. It's not that they're incapable of social interaction. They can be the most social people in the world. It's the energy drain that's holding them back.

He knew that he had to do something. His old technique simply wasn't up to the job. He was paying too high of a price for whatever little he got.

I talked with John through this process and I helped him work through his issues. His issue was not the fact that he is an introvert. You can't choose being an introvert or an extrovert. That's not something for you to choose.

That's like choosing to be right-handed over being left-handed. Sure, you can be born left handed and try to train your right hand, but you're still left handed. That is your nature. There's no need to apologize for that. There's no need to be ashamed of it.

This book is dedicated to people like John because this book is a product of my interactions with him as I helped him work through his issue.

The issue is not him being introverted instead of being an extrovert. Instead, the issue was his coping mechanism.

You see, he was trying to be an extrovert instead of being himself. He was trying to play the role of an extrovert when he should have invested all that time and energy in cultivating basic people skills that would work with his introversion. These are not necessarily mutually exclusive.

Like I said earlier, a lot of introverted people are very social. They have the social skills. They're capable of interacting on a person to person, human to human level. That is not the issue.

The problem that they keep running into is that they're using the wrong method. They think that they have to turn their back on being an introvert and become something they're not.

This book helps introverts with basic people skills. It also helps people, regardless of how busy they are.

A lot of folks are under the impression that you have to spend a tremendous amount of time, resource and energy building up people skills. It's like you're going to some sort of bootcamp.

That's not true. Even if you're very busy and time is a luxury to you, you can pick up these basic people skills and continue to polish them regardless of where you are. There's always an opportunity to connect with people on a one to one basis and build up your skills.

Chapter 1: Why Do Introverts Need to Bother with Basic People Skills?

A lot of introverts are very gifted people. A lot of introverts have higher than average IQs and know how to figure out a situation. They're that intelligent.

Given that native intelligence, it's not a surprise that a lot of introverted people tend to be successful. Given this context, are basic people skills even needed when life is already rewarding them?

Unfortunately, this is just part of the equation. What about introverted people who are still starting in their careers? What about introverted people who have average intelligence and average levels of success? What about introverted people who are busy but success is elusive?

Regardless of what you have built up for yourself and regardless of the rewards life has already given you, it helps to have basic people skills. If anything, it opens the door to richer and more meaningful human to human connections.

Please understand that the source of happiness on this planet is not the stuff you have. Your joy normally doesn't come from the goods you have managed to amass.

Indeed, according to a fairly recent research study, the joy that we get from possessions is not permanent. In fact, in many cases, it's oh so temporary.

It's like you buy a Mercedes Benz, you get all excited, and then your neighbors see your new car. What do you think happens next? That's right, after a few months, somebody else rolls in with a new Mercedes Benz.

And, given enough time, a lot of other people in your area will have similar new cars. That sense of uniqueness that you felt goes away, and you start thinking of buying yet another car.

This is the nature of possessions. You can replace the Mercedes Benz with a handbag or a new outfit. It all goes back to the same psychological root.

The human mind is geared towards novelty. And when the novelty wears off, you're looking for something bigger, brighter and better. It never ends.

This is why the research study concluded that, according to their analysis, people who invest in experiences, maybe it's school, maybe it's a vacation, maybe it's some sort of training program, are happier for a longer period of time.

While it is true that, at a certain level, money does buy happiness, it is equally true that the happiness you buy is temporary. There is a limit to the joy you get from the things you can buy.

Happiness, ultimately, can be found in other people. Happiness, joy and contentment are built on the foundations of the roots you set down and the connections you make with other people around you.

This requires basic people skills. You can't just enter into a room and think that people would automatically understand where you're coming from. It doesn't work that way.

You have to make the effort. You have to make yourself available. Most importantly, you have to be willing, ready and able to reach out and try to understand others.

In other words, seek to understand others first, instead of automatically assuming that people can and should understand you.

Achieve Greater Success and Happiness Through Connections

Let's get one thing clear, society today places a higher value on extrovert skills. When people see that you're open, accessible, willing to cooperate, willing to share ideas, and simply allowing yourself to be available, you are more attractive.

People feel that they can approach you better. You find yourself in more social circles. This makes a lot more things possible for you.

Now, please understand that these are skills. You don't necessarily have to be an extrovert.

You don't necessarily have to change yourself to become somebody you're not. You just have to assume the skills of an extrovert or skills that people normally associate with an extrovert personality. This is very different from pretending to be an extrovert or faking it until you make it.

It's All About Achieving Common Goals

When you look at any kind of social or business organization, it doesn't matter what type of organization it is, the way these human groups define success always involve some sort of common goal.

The key is to get different members of the social unit to do their part so everybody achieves more towards a common goal. This requires interpersonal skills. This also puts a lot of pressure on these organizations to hire only people who can get them to where they want to collectively go.

If you want to have a more successful career and if you want to have a greater impact on whatever group you're in, it's really important to build people skills.

Please understand that having people skills doesn't necessarily mean that you're automatically liked or you're the most popular person in your group. You just need to develop a high enough level of people skills so you can do your part.

Everybody's entitled to their personality. Just because you have people skills, it doesn't necessarily mean that people would think that you are the most popular or most liked person in the group. These don't necessarily have to go hand in hand.

The key is to do your share and to be able to communicate in such a way that you help the group achieve its objective.

You Don't Have to Give Up on Who You Are

If you are reading this book, there's a very high chance you are an introvert. After all, this book is geared towards introverted individuals.

The good news is that you don't have to give up on your introversion. You don't have to reprogram yourself or turn your back on who you really are. You are who you are.

Again, there's nothing to apologize for. There's nothing to be ashamed of. The key here is to embrace your orientation.

You are an introvert. Stop being embarrassed about it. Stop wishing and hoping that you were somebody else or something else.

The first step to developing solid people skills is to begin where you are. For that to happen, you have to accept who you are. You're an introvert.

That designation alone brings a lot of gifts. You're more likely to think before you talk. You're more likely to process connections between the concepts people share when they talk.

You don't have to fake it until you make it. Most importantly, you don't have to feel bad about being an introvert.

The key here is to use your unique gifts as an introvert, namely your ability to think deeply, to give you the mental firepower you need to figure out social skills.

Use your brain power to figure out the social skills you need, not only just to get along with the people in the group, but to thrive in it.

This book will step you through the process of figuring out basic people skills and create a system that enables you to improve your skills over time.

Please understand that your ability to get along with others and communicate effectively to others are your greatest assets. It's time to build up the value of those assets.

Chapter 2: You can Build Up Your People Skills Even if You're Busy

A lot of people are under the impression that they simply don't have the time for people skills. Either they have it or they don't. If they don't, they will just make do with whatever depressed or substandard people skills they have.

The problem with this thinking is that the more you believe that you are too busy to develop people skills, the longer it will take for you to adopt the solution. The problem will persist because you feel that you simply don't have the time to come up with the solution.

Another misconception people have about introverts is that they're plain lazy. The thinking is that since introverts are introspective, they're basically just daydreaming and may be just too busy being so preoccupied to fix their problem.

Well, it's not really a problem. The issue here is one of orientation and positioning.

Introverts are not lazy. They're just oriented a certain way. They're inward-focused.

You can use this to your advantage. You can turn your introspection on certain issues and redirect that focus on both figuring out how people behave in a social setting and understanding the signals involved and the timing required.

Putting all this information together, you can then work with people based on what you have observed.

Of course, a lot of this would be hit or miss. Sometimes, it will be awkward. Sometimes the effect would be magnified by the fact that you are inward-looking.

But you can work your way through this. Just because you're an introvert, it doesn't mean that you give yourself an excuse to not even try.

A lot of introverts are actually their worst enemies. They think that there's something wrong with them because they just keep themselves or they spend a lot more time thinking about something instead of verbalizing it or acting on it.

Well, these are actually strengths, if you think about it. Does it really make sense to blurt something out and then later on have to walk it back? Is it really all that productive to jump in with both feet when you still haven't really fully analyzed what exactly you are getting into?

I can't even begin to tell you how many relationships are destroyed by people who were just too quick on the trigger. They feel that the world owes them something, or at least owes them enough to automatically understand what they're saying.

The world doesn't work that way. You have a lot of responsibility.

Because when you say something out of turn or say something that's not fully thought out, there will be consequences. Feelings will be hurt. Decisions may take longer. People might feel marginalized or insulted. Worse yet, people might get false hopes.

All of these have consequences. All of these have costs. There's a lot to recommend introspection. There's a lot of value in being introverted.

The Key to Overcoming the Social Limitations of Introversion

The key to solving your people skills issue is not lack of intelligence. Like I said, a lot of introverts are quite intelligent people. The issue is confidence in your capabilities.

You don't have to feel like you are a fish out of water when you're dealing with people and getting along well with them. It doesn't have to be a drain on you. It also doesn't have to be a crushing experience.

Please understand that setbacks happen all the time. I'm sure the first time you swung that bat, you did not hit a home run. Very few people do. What's important is you got up to try again and again.

Celebrate the grit that you develop. Feel good about the capabilities you have and the fact that you've given yourself this opportunity to get out there and build people skills.

It may seem awkward, it may be a touch and go affair most of the time, but that's just part of the territory. What's important is you need to stop giving yourself reasons to not even try.

Drop the "I am too busy" Excuse

Now, I'm going to the meat and potatoes of this chapter. This book is written for busy introverts. But let's get one thing clear: if you want to find the time, you will find it. Seriously.

If you don't believe me, list down everything you do in the span or an 8-hour work day. If you slice and dice that data with all honesty, you'd be surprised to find out that, at most, you are working 30-40% of the time or less.

In other words, you put in 8 hours, but your productive time is, at best, 3 to 4 hours. No joke. This is called the Pareto Principle.

If you haven't heard of that term, it's also called the 80/20 rule. This rule says that 80% of your output was produced by 20% of your time.

That 8 hours that you spend at work, most of it is fluff. You know it. And I suspect other people know it as well. Your boss definitely knows it because your boss knows that this applies across the board.

Where does 80% of your time go? It goes to non-essential stuff like shuffling papers around, talking with people around the water cooler, sending emails, checking updates, and so on and so forth.

I raise this basic productivity fact with you to clue you in on where your time is going to come from. Knowing that the 80/20 rule is in effect, this means that if you only focus on the 20% that's producing 80% of your results and doubled that time, you end up with a 60% improvement in the results that you're getting. Isn't that awesome? Best of all, you still have 60% of free time.

This is why you really cannot say with all honesty that you're simply too busy to pick up on people skills. You definitely can't use your introversion as an excuse.

I want you to start freeing up time off your "busy schedule." It doesn't have to be big. You don't have to be a hero at first. You can just start with freeing up 10 minutes, then scaling it up to 15, then 20, then half an hour.

Don't panic. There's a lot more where that came from if you apply the Pareto Principle to your typical work day.

Most of our time is filled with "fluff" activities. There's definitely time there if you are willing to squeeze. So, find the time.

Don't say that you're just too busy to do this because this book is structured in such a way that you will be able to pick up people skills wherever you are, whenever you are, and practice them consistently and constantly, even if you don't have that much time.

See you in Chapter 3.

Chapter 3: 7 People Skills Every Busy Introvert Should Know

In this chapter, I'm going to give you a quick rundown of the 7 skills that this book is going to teach you. I'm going to go into some detail regarding these skills, why they're necessary, how they work, as well as a step by step guide that enables you to acquire them.

Please understand that all the skills that you will learn from this book require constant practice. You can't just think about these skills and, for whatever reason, everything falls into place. They don't work like that.

You actually have to challenge yourself constantly and consistently to hone these skills. Certain things may make sense on paper, but if you actually carry them out in real life situations, then you will see how they work with where you are.

Different people are at different stages and at different levels as far as their social skills go. There's nothing wrong with this. There's nothing to apologize about. You are who you are and you are where you are.

Everybody's different. Everybody has different backgrounds. Everybody has different experiences. Accordingly, you have to fine tune, tweak and modify these steps so you can develop these skills in your specific context.

Nobody can tell you, through the form of a book, where you are exactly and what kind of specific steps you need to take. You can only follow a framework, and then fill in the details.

You have to play it by ear to a certain extent. But the good news is, the following materials will give you enough of a starting framework so you can put together something that works for you right here, right now.

There's no one size fits all, cookie cutter solution. You have to fill in the details because you're the one who has to live this out based on the specific situations in your life.

With that out of the way, here is the quick overview of the 7 skills you will be learning from this book.

Effective Communication Skills

To be able to get your message across is fundamental to people skills. This is the bedrock of all other skills. I'll step you through some basic techniques that would enable you to improve your ability to get your message across.

Again, this works with where you are. I don't assume some sort of ideal standard that you have already reached. Anybody can apply these steps. After all, there's always room for improvement.

Active Listening Skills

Learning to listen to other people is a crucial skill in getting along more effectively and efficiently with others. There is such a thing as active listening.

A lot of people think that as long as they know how to hear sounds, they are automatically listening. Absolutely wrong.

When you listen actively to other people, you make them feel more at ease, and this enables both of you to communicate better. This allows for an honest, open and easier communication.

Negotiation Skills

Every single day you meet other people, your negotiation skills will be tested. That's the bottom line.

Whenever you make a request, whenever you ask for something, there will be an opportunity for you to develop your negotiation skills further.

There will always be situations where you need other people to do something for you. Maybe they're obligated to do this. Oftentimes, they're not.

Whenever there are two egos involved, there is always a possibility of conflict.

Regardless of how you slice and dice it, there's always going to be a need for negotiation skills.

Being more effective with people requires your ability to negotiate despite differences so you can contribute to the success of the larger group that you find yourself in, build higher quality relationships, get the very best deals you're capable of, and otherwise resolve issues.

Personal Problem-Solving Skills

Whenever you're working in any social setting, there is bound to be a problem. This problem doesn't necessarily have to involve other people or groups of people. This doesn't have to involve some sort of intra-group or inter-group issue. This can be a simple matter of people not being able to figure out how to do things or their group is doing something and you run into some sort of technical impasse.

Being able to solve problems is not just an individual skill. It has a social dimension. Being able to offer the right solution at the right time can help your group avoid any injury, loss, or prevent problems before they even happen.

Learn to Encourage and Motivate Others

Every group of people requires cohesion. It also requires proper motivation for everybody to live up to their fullest potential.

Sadly, too many people think that they already know how to encourage and motivate others. What they don't realize is that oftentimes, they're doing these things on a very inefficient basis. They can be doing a much better job.

In this section, I'm going to step you through the process of motivating and encouraging others in a more effective and efficient way.

Developing and Nurturing Your Personal Flexibility and Open-mindedness

Nothing causes social friction more than sticking to your guns and being stubborn. Just because you can see certain patterns, it doesn't necessarily mean that the outcome would be a foregone conclusion.

Unfortunately, too many people have this attitude and that's why they find themselves in the middle of unnecessary social conflict.

By learning to cultivate your natural tendency towards flexibility and open-mindedness, you allow yourself to grow as a person in a social setting. Not only would you learn more, but you will get along better with others.

Cultivating a Good Sense of Humor

Let's face it, we live in an imperfect world where life is often chaotic. We can look at life as an unending series of tragedies, with certain pauses and breaks in between. On the other hand, we can look at it with a decent dose of humor and roll with the punches.

Please understand that when you develop this social skill, you are able to set people at ease more easily. This enables others to be more comfortable around you, and this mutual comfort makes you a more effective communicator.

Chapter 4: 5-Step Formula for Effective Communication Skills

It's easy to think that when you open your mouth and words come out, that you are automatically communicating to others. After all, you are thinking certain concepts, verbalizing them, and using air vibrations to communicate those thoughts. Seems pretty straightforward and basic.

The problem is, there is more going on in effective human to human, person to person communications than mere sound vibrations.

You have to not just focus on the things you can hear, but also on the things that you cannot hear. I'm talking about nonverbal signals. I'm talking about context. I'm talking about the actual exchange that you have with another person.

Please understand that the words that you use to communicate make up only half of your message. You still have to account for the other half.

You still have to be careful of the total message you are communicating. Otherwise, it's very easy to spend a lot more time trying to get your message across because you didn't quite do a good job the first time around.

Also, becoming a more effective communicator enables you to be more persuasive. You are able to rally people to your cause. You're able to convince people to do what you'd like them to do.

At the very least, you can open their minds to the possibility of the option that you bring to the table. That's very hard to do if you just think that communication is just simply getting certain words out.

If you rely on other people to understand you, then you are putting too much power in their hands. You have to craft your message in such a way that it has a better average chance of convincing others, or at least opening their minds.

Another reason why you need to brush up on your communication skills is the fact that we often communicate in a way that leads to confusion.

You can't just assume that just because your mental image of the idea you're trying to communicate is so crisp, vivid and sharp that the person at the other end of the conversation would automatically get that picture. They won't.

We all have different barriers or filters that get in the way. There's the cultural barrier, and there's the personal barrier with all its different experiences. There's also the context barrier. Some people are busy, some people are distracted.

When you add all of these up, you can't automatically assume that because the message is clear and accurate on your end that it would be perceived automatically the same way at the other end. This requires attention to detail. This requires stepping up your communication skills so you're less likely to be misunderstood.

Finally, effective communication skills also involve communicating with a certain level of assertiveness.

Please understand that people are looking for guidance. They don't like wishy-washy people. They don't like people who don't fully believe in their position or who are uncertain.

They'd rather not waste time on people who are saying certain things that they themselves are unsure of. In other words, they're looking for a certain level of certainty and confidence.

Unfortunately, even if you were speaking nothing but the truth, if you don't say it in an assertive way, you're giving people reason to doubt your sincerity and the truthfulness of what you just said or other issues.

This is very distracting because this takes the focus away from discussing the actual meat and potatoes of what you said.

People are wasting a tremendous intellectual and social capital trying to figure out the basics of what you're saying because they really can't quite trust you. You seem so wishy-washy and weak.

Effective Communication is Crucial Regardless of Form

Whether you're writing to somebody or you're talking to them face to face, you need to communicate clearly. This is crucial in any kind of context.

Whether you're trying to build better relationships, whether you're trying to make new friends and acquaintances, or whether you are trying to get some business done, you have to have solid communication skills.

Indeed, in a study done by Robert Half Management Resources, a survey of 1,000 American workers showed that effective communication and matching diplomacy are the key skills management needs to have for a more effective working relationship with their employees.

Indeed, in the same study, almost a third of employee respondents said that their boss simply did not meet their standards of effective communications.

This is crucial because if you are in an organization and you want people to achieve common goals, you have to communicate clearly. Otherwise, basic issues like priorities, workplace obstructions, workloads, as well as quality expectations, may mean different things between employees and managers.

There are many managers who automatically assume that they are communicating effectively when it turns out that their employees can't really understand where they're coming from or figure out their priorities.

The end result is a feeling of disengagement. Employees often feel alienated or isolated from the overall process at work. This leads to lower productivity and lower work quality.

Effective Communication Requires Active Management of its Nonverbal Components

As I have mentioned earlier in this chapter, when you communicate with people, they're not just paying attention to the sounds that your mouth is making. They're also paying attention to your facial expressions, your gestures, your body language, even what you're wearing.

All of these paint a complete picture. And this picture is not just something you can hear.

Accordingly, to become a more effective communicator, you have to present a vivid 3-dimensional picture. This way, all signals coming from you, whether they be verbal or nonverbal, are consistent. These signals then serve to reinforce the message your verbal communication pushes forward.

Be aware of these seemingly minor details.

Believe or not, whether you touch somebody while you talk, the timing in which you introduce a certain topic, the way you move your body, how quickly you talk, as well as your matching facial expressions, gestures as well as postures, go a long way in either undermining or strengthening the point you are making with your verbal communications.

Why is Nonverbal Communications More Important?

Believe it or not, scientific studies show that nonverbal communication is actually more important than verbal communication.

This throws a lot of people for a loop because it's very easy to conclude that your verbal message is more important because it's easier to figure out.

This is not the case. People actually pick up on your nonverbal communication faster than your verbal message. In fact, it's the first thing they perceive.

They think they can figure you out a mile away. You haven't even opened your mouth and they already get an impression of the message you are trying to communicate.

In a study conducted in the 1970s by a psychology professor Albert Mehrabian, a comprehensive study of other research papers on effective communications demonstrate that only 7% of the total signals people send involve the actual literal content of people's communication.

On top of this, 38% of the perceived message is accounted for by voice volume, intonation, and the tone of one's voice. These are all voice factors.

Finally, the other 55% of the person's communicated message is made up of body language.

This important research shows that to become a more effective communicator, you have to pay attention to the total package you are projecting.

It's too easy to get all caught up in the information that you have to share. Maybe you're sharing data. Maybe you are trying to communicate the findings of some exciting research.

However, if you notice that people are getting bored or people keep asking you the same question over and over again, this means that you're not getting through.

Whatever clarity and excitement you may be feeling on your end is simply not getting across to the people you're trying to reach. This is due to the fact that you haven't looked at the complete package that you bring to the table.

Pay attention to how you talk. Pay attention to how you stand and the placement of your arms, the tone of your voice, your facial gesture, and how wide your eyes are as you emphasize certain words. All these and many other details present a complete picture.

Remember, the target audience is only perceiving 7% of your message. You have to take responsibility for and closely manage the other 93% that they are not hearing. These are the things that they see and otherwise perceive. One important way to do this is to know your audience and its preferences.

In a 1990 study conducted among Stanford University graduate students, 80 students were split up into two roughly equal groups.

One group was instructed to finger tap three popular songs for the other group who is tasked to simply listen. The tappers were then asked to estimate the percentage of their listeners correctly identifying the tune they're tapping out.

The listeners, on the other hand, understood that they're going to be guessing the tune that their tapping partner was tapping out. The researchers instructed the listeners to write down their guesses after they listened to the tapped-out tune.

Both partners were specifically instructed not to communicate anything to each other except the tapping. They're not to talk to each other until the exercise was over. In fact, they were seated back to back so they don't see each other.

After this session, the experimenters then told the pairs that they should estimate how many of an audience of 100 listeners would correctly identify the tune if the tapping sound was projected to a recital hall. It turns out that only 2.5% of all guesses were correct.

This study indicates the big disconnect between the signals people send and their expectations. In other words, we think that people are more likely to get our message accurately when it turns out that there's a lot of room of improvement.

We all have filters in different contexts. And this is why it's really important to get a clear understanding of all the different variables involved so we can become more effective communicators.

Step by Step Instructions for Boosting Your Communication Skills

Step #1: Sign up for as many communication tasks you have access to

It doesn't matter whether you're in school or you're already working. Look for opportunities where you are going to be presenting something to other people.

Maybe it's a meeting, maybe it's a study group, or it's a form of presentation, it doesn't matter. What's important is you expose yourself to as many of these opportunities as possible.

When you do this, you are forced to prepare your speech ahead of time. This means that you're going to have to come up with a plan.

First of all, you have to identify what your goals are. What is your desired outcome for the speech?

Second, you are going to outline what you're going to say. You can prepare a typed-out speech, but it's not going to be as good as a speech that you use talking points for.

When you present a speech that you just read out, a lot is lost in translation. The key point here is to practice your ability to talk using key discussion points so you can further refine the mix of verbal and nonverbal signals you are projecting to your audience.

By going through this process several times, you also build your own personal competence as far as effective communications go. You become more confident about your ability to communicate the right message at the right time, with the right people in the right context.

Step #2: When talking to others, get straight to the point

Another helpful skill that you can consistently practice is to strip down your basic communications with others.

It's very easy to get lost in the details. It's very easy to just become so comfortable with the other person that you go off from one tangent to the next.

The problem here is, when that happens, you're not really building your ability to communicate in a clear and direct way.

The better approach would be to get straight to the point first, and then ask the person you're talking to several questions that help you figure out if they got your message right the first time around. Once you're satisfied, then you can shoot the bull with that person.

Don't start with chitchat. Focus first on getting your message across and use this as a reference point to help you fine tune your communication skills.

Step #3: Know and prepare for your audience

Take every opportunity to talk to people. Understand that whether you are speaking to one person or to a hundred people, you're talking to an audience. Try to figure out what your audience would expect and change your communication positioning accordingly.

It's a bad idea to talk to a business client like you would talk to your sales manager and vice versa. I'm not just talking about the content of your verbal communications. I'm also talking about your tone, your timing, the way you position your body, your facial expressions and gestures.

Understand that different combinations of nonverbal signals are required, depending on who your audience is.

Step #4: Avoid annoying other people

I know this is kind of a weird piece of advice, but let's face it, there are many people on this planet that simply do not like how we talk.

They don't know us, so it's not personal. For whatever reason, you just trip them up. They just become instinctively annoyed.

Instead of worrying yourself sick with the idea that, somehow, you can prevent this, focus instead on quickly and efficiently detecting signs of annoyance or irritation. In other words, learn how to detect potential issues so you can make changes in how you present your information so as to turn things around.

Of course, this is not a slam dunk. Nothing is guaranteed. But the good news is, if you know what to look for, you can at least minimize damage or even get a chance to turn things around.

I can't even begin to tell you how many times I've spoken to a large group of people and I thought that the speech was going to end very badly. But I read the reactions I got from the faces in the crowd and made certain changes in how I presented the information, and I ended up with a standing ovation.

You can do the same. Just because they send you initial signals of rejection, skepticism, suspicion and negativity, it doesn't mean that your interaction with them has to stay there. You can turn things around. You have a lot more control over the situation than you give yourself credit for.

Step #5: Emphasize alternative means of communication

Since you're an introvert, please understand that there are nonverbal components to effective communication.

By definition, you are a nonverbal person, so this is good news for you. Instead of obsessing about or feeling really insecure about the verbal part, take comfort and confidence from the fact that the verbal component of any effective person to person communication is only 7%.

You can master the nonverbal portions. These require a little bit more deliberation. They greatly reward thinking before you talk.

You can be more intentional as far as these elements are concerned. You can put a lot more of your intellectual firepower in positioning yourself so as to maximize the effect of these nonverbal signals.

Please understand that when it comes to effective communication, volume is not everything. There's a lot to recommend the old Zen Buddhist saying of "Less is more."

What if I told you that the most effective communicators don't speak all that much? They say very little, but the words that they do manage to get across carries so much weight. They are able to persuade people better. They are able to pack so much meaning in such a few words. You can do the same.

Don't get scared stiff of finding the right words, speaking in front of people you may not know all that well, and the other situations that you are struggling with. Instead, focus on your strengths.

You can spend quite a bit of time making sure that you're properly dressed and that you're sending the right nonverbal signals. You can practice your facial expressions as well as your gestures in front of a mirror. You can also scope out the venue that you're going to speak in.

You have a lot more control over the situation than it appears.

Chapter 5: Step-By-Step Process About How To Listen Actively

Just like with effective verbal communication most people think that they are already listening correctly. They automatically assume that if their ears can pick up the sounds other people make that they by definition are listening. That's completely wrong. There is a difference between listening and hearing. Unless you are deaf or you have physical issues with your ear, you would know how to hear. That's not the problem.

The problem is, hearing is very different from listening. Make no mistake. If you want to brush up your people's skills, you have to learn how to listen to others. It's not as easy as you think. The big hurdle is ego.

Please understand that you have one mouth and two ears. It's probably a good idea to use your mouth less and hear more often. In fact, there's an old saying attributed to US President Calvin Coolidge. The saying goes "No man has listen his way out of a job." When in doubt, shut up and listen. That's how effective listening is, because you can learn how to figure somebody out.

Oftentimes as I have mentioned in the chapter regarding effective communication skills, 7% of the total message you're sending out is communicated to verbal signals. The rest involves non-verbal communication and this is where listening comes in.

You see when you actively listen to somebody, you get the total context of what they're saying. You're not just hearing their words. Because if effective listening is all about hearing it can be reduce to mere hearing then you won't need to be in front of another person. Seriously. You can just send audio to each other and call it a day. It doesn't work that way.

If you've ever been into a job interview, you'll know full well how this works out. You can say the right answers to the right questions and think you did awesome. In fact you may think you killed it. But then you call back and they tell you that they'll call you, don't call them. What went wrong? Well, it all boils down to the fact that effective listening and effective communication involves more than just the actual sound signals being send out. It also involves context.

In this chapter, I'm going to walk you through the process of learning how to listen actively. This means you have to concentrate. Figure out the context and subtext of what the person is communicating. Just because you can both understand English, doesn't mean that that's the beginning in the end of your conversations.

There's a lot more going on.

Because two people may speak the same language and they may be just using the same words but mean completely different things.

A great listener is able to understand the context of what the other person is saying and go beyond the surface meaning of the words. As an active listener, you figure out the context, the subtext and the motivation behind the words being spoken to you. Please understand that as rich and varied as the English language is, there's a reason why people use certain words and not others.

When you're an active listener you get a new ones understanding of these strategic choices. Of course, as you hone your ability to read between the lines and listen intently to the context of what's being said, you pick up on the skill as you go along. It's not something that you can put your finger on and say, "This is what's happening" and clearly delineate a different context as they present themselves to you. It's not that obvious nor is it black and white. This is the kind of skills that you develop after you have listened to a wide range of people in a wide range context at different times.

Patience Required

How do you become an active listener?

The first thing that you need is patience. It takes a long time to figure out people. It's not like that there is some sort of manual that says, " When this person says this, this is what they really mean", or "If they say it in this particular tone, this is what they mean". It would be great if such manual exist. But unfortunately, that manual doesn't exist. You have to deal with people as they are, where they are, when you meet them.

In other words this is the kind of skill that you pick up over time in a task accumulative effect. It doesn't come fully formed. It doesn't fall from the sky straight into your lap. That's definitely not something you stumble upon. It is a skill set that you have to actively seek out, master over an extended period of time. It kind of grows on you. But make no mistakes. Its power utility and value scale up exponentially.

In other words, a little bit of time, effort and focus invested in this particular skill pays off handsomely for the rest of your life.

Part of a reason why a lot of people are not as effective as they could be when it comes to interpersonal communications is because they haven't really lived up to their fullest listening capacity. They're capable of so much more but they think that they already have everything figured out so they remain stuck. Too bad! Because if you really want to be an effective leader, a more understanding person and more likable person across the board, you have to listen.

And the toughest part is that you have to take the initiative because most people have the sound of their voice. Most of us would love to get on that soapbox and hug the spotlight. But the problem is, when you're talking, you're not learning. When you're talking, you're the one trying to teach people but if you really want to learn from and figure somebody out, you have to sit back and take it. This is where listening comes in.

In a study released in 1995 in the journal "Psychological Bulletin" found that human beings are able to connect better when they feel that they belong. And this initial research opened a very important gateway into how crucial the sense of belonging is. And one key social exercise that fosters the sense of belonging is the perception that were somehow connected. This is where listening comes in.

When you're truly listening to somebody, you are able to connect on an emotional, intellectual and psychological basis. You may not be able to fully understand the other person but it's obvious to them that you're at least reaching out and trying to connect with them at a much deeper level than normal. With everything else being equal the standard modern day connection that people gets is not all that deep. We're often stuck at business transactions. It's very easy to dismiss our interpersonal interactions solely on the basis of numbers. Either you're making money from somebody else or somebody else is making money from you, it's essentially stuck at the level of business transaction.

When people feel that you're actually reaching out and listening to them, even though the context is commercial, you trigger that sense of connectivity which leads to what most people need. Most people need that they belong. Most people need to feel that they matter or that they are important. That they have meaning and purpose on this planet. That's the gateway that effective listening skills bring to the table. It's hard to make somebody feel that they belong when all you do is talk at them. The chances of that happening are quite remote.

What's more effective is when you sit back and allow them to take the spotlight. Belonging enables people to feel empowered. And what do you think happens when you enable people to feel that they belong? They are more apt to like you. They are more likely to be comfortable around you and this can deepen your social relationship.

Active listening is more than paying attention. It's very easy to confuse active listening with the act of paying attention. It's very easy to think that these are one and the same. The problem with paying attention is that it just uses one of your senses. I think you know which sense this is. Obviously it involves your hearing. But outside of that,   nothing   else   is   registering.

When you pay attention to somebody, you use all your senses. In other words, when somebody is making a point you reiterate the total attention you're giving that person by referencing another sense.

For example, somebody is making a point and you say to that person, "I feel you." When you say that, you reference your tack tile sense, your ability to touch. And perceive the world through your sense of touch. You can also say, "I see your point." Again this is a form of encouragement because you communicate to the person on a subliminal basis that "I might just hearing the point that you're saying." This goes beyond that. "I'm actually understanding the full complexity and the new ones to the point that you're trying to get across. And it impacts me so much that I can actually perceive it in more than an auditory way. I can figuratively see it or feel it." This again triggers the sense of connectivity between two people and this can act as a gateway to a sense of belonging.

One way to communicate this deep level of connection in the context of active listening is through mimicry. In a study in the journal

"Psychological Science" published in January 2004, researchers split up participants into two groups. For one group, the researchers' going to mimic the body language of the participants they are going to give a sales presentation to.

For the control group the researcher is not going to make any mimicry. After the researcher mimicked the experimental group's action, the researcher "accidentally drop items in the ground". It turns out that the people in the experimental group were more likely to be generous and helpful to the researcher than the non-mimicked or control group. The experimental would drop the items on the ground and if the person wasn't helped within 10 seconds, the experimenter would pick up the items   herself.

This study showed that when people feel a sense of connection through previous interaction with another person, they are more likely to have positive feelings about that person which translate to better cooperation as well as willingness to help that individual. This highlights the importance of connecting through active listening.

What if I told you that by simply repeating or paraphrasing what the other person is saying to you, you communicate in clear terms your interest in what they have to say. This is a very important factor because a lot of observers easily dismiss this. They think that just because you're talking to somebody that you're automatically interested in what they have to say. This is not true. In fact, people often find themselves talking over each other. You're not really listening. You're basically just exchanging sounds.

When you paraphrase and repeat, you communicate to that other person that "Yes, I'm intently, mentally figuring out what you're saying and I'm bouncing it up back to you for your concurrence if anything else." In other words, by doing this simple exercise you ensure that you're both on the same page.

In a January 6, 2010 article published in the "Journal of Listening" a hundred eighty (180) students participated in peer interviews, where they were given either a simple acknowledgment of their expressed opinion or a paraphrase. They were then asked to share what they thought about the interviewer. The students who were simply given an acknowledgment for their shared opinion didn't show a dramatic increase in their perceived likability of the interviewer. This was completely opposite of the paraphrase group.

The study highlights the fact that when we get some sort of acknowledgment in the form paraphrase, the acknowledgment of the attention we're getting in the form of paraphrasing, we are more likely to feel connected, and we're more likely to have positive feelings towards the person we are interacting with.

Step by step Instructions

Step 1: Consciously focus your complete attention to the speaker

When somebody is talking, don't just pay attention to the words they're saying. Try to figure out their emotional state. Try to map out how they came up with their train of thought. In other words, try to understand the internal logic of what they are saying.

Some people are very visual so they can diagram what other people are saying. Other people are more auditory. So basically, statements tend to flow with each other. Regardless of how your mind is oriented, dig deep. And try to look beyond the words the person is using.

Step 2. Show your attention

Demonstrate your attention with non-verbal ques. Raise your eyebrows Nod your head. Rub your chin. Look to the side and look like you're thinking deeply. Also make sounds that indicate that the words that they are saying is resonating with you at some level. Create an overall picture that they are connecting with you on so many different   levels.

Of course this has to be sincere. You actually have to be listening to what they're saying. It has to connect with you. What you are doing in this exercise is brushing up on your non-verbal vocabulary so you can get that message of connectedness   across   loud   and   clear.

Step 3. Paraphrase what the other person is   saying.

It's important to break the dialog from time to time by paraphrasing what the other person is saying. When you do this, you make sure that you communicate to that person. That you are on the same page or at least are trying to be on the same page. They may correct you. Maybe you misunderstood a little bit of what they are saying.

Regardless, this goes a long way in saying to that person "Yes, I'm trying to connect with you. You can develop a sense of belonging with me because I'm actually listening intently to you in more ways or one."

You can easily paraphrase by saying, "So you're saying that...." And then repeat the summary of what they are saying in your own words. This shows that at the very least you are trying to understand where that person is coming from and what they're saying.

Step 4. Ask open ended questions

Whenever you're engage in a two way discussion with somebody, don't kill the discussion by asking "yes or no" questions. Instead focus on open ended questions that would help them dig deeper or explore other areas of their main point.

The idea here is to not only foster s deeper level mutual comfort but also uncover or expose hidden meanings. Maybe they're just not doing a good job explaining what they really want to say or that there are other issues. They may want to acknowledge took themselves so you're kind of helping them work through the real issue.

Step 5. Don't butt-in just for the sake of filling the silence

Please understand that whenever you're talking with other people, there will be quiet moments. Don't automatically assume that this quiet moments are awkward or oft putting. In many cases it's the absence of sounds that make the impact of their previous statements more powerful. Let the words sink in. Look at this gaps as punctuation points for an effective conversation. Don't automatically assume that if there is a gap of several minutes that the situation is awkward and you have to proactively try to "fix" the conversation.

Effective listening is partly about unlocking the power of silence. Just because somebody stopped talking, doesn't mean they stop communicating. They're communicating out with you by looking at you. Maybe they are smiling. Maybe they're having facial expression.

Maybe they're on gesture. Understand that this is happening because you can communicate that "word pause" with you facial expressions, body language or other non-verbal signals. Don't automatically assume that completely stopped communicating just because the other person has stopped talking. Effective listening is all about continuing to draw out information and sharing information to that person in a non-verbal way.

Chapter 6: Negotiation And Conflict Resolution Skills Are Easier Than You Thought

The term "negotiation" actually has a broader meaning than most people care to realize. It's very easy to define negotiation as involving two people who want totally different things, trying to meet somewhere in the middle.

It is also often popularly defined as involving deal-making, or trying to get more favorable terms from another person who may not necessarily want to give such terms. But there's actually a lot more to negotiation than these common definitions bring to the table.

Negotiation really involves the ability to work with people whenever there's any kind of conflict. When you are looking for a low price, and the buyer only wants a high price, there's a conflict there. Your interests don't line up.

When you're trying to request something from somebody, you're going to have to convince that person, because they may not be all that motivated to give you what you're looking for. It's important to understand that negotiation covers all of these.

Because if you think that negotiation is just all about business, or trying to get the best deal possible, you're missing out. You won't put yourself in a situation where you will be fully developing this skill set. Make no mistake, whenever you're dealing with any person on this planet, your negotiation skills will be tested.

This is the good news. In other words, every time you interact with another human being, you can brush up on your negotiation skills. You can take things to the next level by practicing it with everyone you meet, in any context, and at any time.

Introverts And Negotiation Skills

Since you're an introvert, you may think that negotiation is going to take a lot out of you. It's hard enough interacting with people socially because of the energy it requires. It's very easy to add a layer of intimidation to this by necessarily defining negotiation as a zero-sum game.

In other words, for your slice of the pie to get bigger, you're going to have to talk to somebody else into giving up their slice of the pie. In other words, victory can only be attained at the expense of another person. Somebody has to lose for you to win.

Negotiation excellence doesn't have to lead to win-lose situations. There is such a thing as a win-win situation. A rising tide, after all, lifts all boats. Just because you're used to cutting up a pie, and somebody else's slice necessarily gets smaller, there's still the possibility of both of you working together to increase the size of the pie so there's more for everybody.

Effective negotiation also involves those scenarios. Keep this in mind, because it all boils down to conflict resolution.

In a study out of the University of California Berkeley, published in the Journal of Personality and Social Psychology in 2007, it was discovered that people who believe that their negotiation skills can be improved over time, tend to be more successful than people who think that negotiation skills are hard-wired, and are somehow attached to certain personality traits that are fixed. This is a conclusion that was derived from several studies.

One of these studies involved participants who were given one of two articles to read. One group of people were assigned an article stating that negotiation ability is changeable and can be developed. The other participants read an article that said negotiation ability, like plaster, is pretty stable over time.

These two groups of participants were then subjected to a battery of negotiation skills tests. The study elicited a conclusion that the belief of the negotiators impacts their outcome, and this initial belief plays a big role in how well they actually perform when they negotiate.

This is why it's crucial to have the right mindset about negotiation coming in. It's not set in stone. You can level up your skills, and there will always be room for improvement. If you believe in these fundamentals, you're more likely to successfully negotiate with another party.

Negotiation is all about give and take

As the phrase itself says, when you negotiate, you're both giving and taking. This is also happening on the other side; it's an exchange. A lot of people are under the impression that this always involves a favorable exchange. In other words, I'm giving what I just want to give and taking what I want, and the same applies to the other side.

If you've done any kind of negotiation in real life, you know that this isn't true. Oftentimes, negotiation means giving up your strong points, or conceding in exchange for some sort of return. It's not always a perfect exchange.

You can theoretically stand on your rights and insist on nothing but the best (the best position or the best outcome), but the problem is if you do that, you probably won't get that exchange to happen in the first place.

To maximize the possibility that people will give up some of their advantages so you can benefit, you have to make the first move. This is called reciprocity. When you're negotiating with another person, it helps if you do that other person an initial favor.

They feel that one good turn deserves another. Since you made the first move, and you took the initiative to benefit them, at some level or another, they feel compelled to return the favor. Use this to your advantage because this is rooted in human nature.

In a study published in the journal Social Influence, out of Santa Clara University in January 2009, researchers explored the question of whether people would reciprocate a favor even if nobody knew if the favor was returned.

One hundred twenty undergraduates were tasked to complete a survey measuring cognitive perceptual skills. This was then followed up by a personality test. The skills test was actually fake. This was just intended to cover up for the personality test.

Participants were randomly assigned to either receive a bottle of water from a confederate of the researcher, or not receive a bottle of water. When the participants were asked to take a survey, they were told that they could take the survey home with them, and then go back to a specific place, at a specific time 2-3 days later.

Half of the study participants thought that the person who gave them the bottle of water would be there to receive their survey results. The other half were told to drop off the survey in a box. Regardless of whether they were dropping off the results in a box, or giving the survey to a person, the people who received the favor of bottled water were more likely to return the survey than those who did not get the favor at all.

This highlights the fact that even if there is no social mechanism involved in verifying if people returned the favor, they are hardwired to return the favor. This is a very powerful study that highlights just how effective reciprocity is as a negotiation tool.

Use it to your full advantage. Whatever small favor you do to the other party can make them more likely to see your position, and at least meet you part of the way there. You may not both get the best outcomes, but the results you get will definitely be much better than if you had both dug in your heels.

Get ready for failed negotiations

A lot of introverts look at negotiation in strictly take-it-or-leave-it terms. They feel that either the negotiations work, or they don't. They think that there is no other alternative. Believe it or not, most negotiations hit a snag. Most negotiation talks don't produce results. It's only when people have a backup plan that things start to materialize.

The actual deals that you hear about in the news are actually plan B's. They weren't the original optimal outcome that people sought coming into the negotiation talks. Please understand that if you want to become a better negotiator despite the fact that you're an introvert, you have to have a backup plan.

Negotiations do fail, but it's still good to have an alternative offer so as to maximize whatever bargaining power you have.

Step by step instructions:

Step #1 : Be upfront when negotiating with people

Whenever you find yourself in any negotiation situation, be upfront. Tell them "This is what I have to offer, and there are going to be no surprises." Because when you lay down your cards, people can see your good will. They don't think that you're trying to pull a fast one. They don't think that you're trying to manipulate them.

Your sincerity shows your clean hands, and people are more likely to take you at face value. This creates a good start for the negotiation process. This enables you to then itemize the issues you want to discuss. Compare this with hiding the ball or talking in generalities.

Since people don't know where you're going to be coming from, you can bet that they're going to try to evade, hide, or even misrepresent.

Step #2 : Focus your negotiations strictly to the issues you are talking about

When you're negotiating, define the points of contention. Don't let the talks bleed over into other issues. For example, if you're talking to your boss about possibly getting a raise, talk about how much money you're getting paid and the skills and experience you bring to the table, as well as the industry trends in your job.

You then talk about how these lead to you being qualified for a new position being created for you, or a new position that actually just opened up in your organization. Stick to the basics, keep it focused. This makes you a more effective negotiator because you lead the conversation, or at least help define its direction.

Step #3 : Offer a favor in advance

For example, when you want to negotiate the hours you spend at work, don't just go into the meeting and ask that your hours be changed. Instead, find an opportune time to do favors for your boss that is outside of your job description. Maybe they wanted you to pick up a bunch of files, and this isn't normally something that you do.

Do something out of the ordinary, and then when you get into the negotiations, you have a little bit of reciprocity power going for you. Please understand that human beings are reciprocal in nature, and if they notice that you did them a favor, they can't help but try to return that favor.

Of course, this all depends on how reasonable your demands are. If you're just looking for a little bit more work schedule flexibility, and not a reduction in your total hours, you probably would get what you're looking for.

Step #4 : Always be ready to suggest alternatives

Do not approach negotiations with a take-it-or-leave-it attitude. Just because your initial ask is not going to happen, doesn't mean that you have to let the negotiations die on that point. Be ready with backup plans. If plan B doesn't work, try C, then D, then E.

In fact, the more backup plans you have, the more you clearly communicate to the other side that you are not unreasonable or inflexible. This puts the onus on them to come up with something equally reasonable.

Step #5 : When you reach an agreement, always ask for documentation or memorialization

Whenever you get a deal with somebody, make sure you get something concrete for it. This occurs in sales settings all the time. Please understand that there are a lot of sales people out there that would tell you what you want to hear just to get a sale, but when the time comes to get them to deliver on the extras you negotiated for, they pretend that your discussion never happened.

They don't pretend that you agreed to the sale, that you bought from them, but they pretend that everything else didn't happen. Don't put yourself in this position. Ask for objective proof by getting it memorialized in one form or another.

Chapter 7: How To Solve Problems In A Group Setting

As an introvert, you already know how to solve problems alone. This is one key definition of introversion; you are more comfortable with ideas than you are with social settings. Be that as it may. To develop effective people skills, you have to learn how to solve problems in a group setting.

Thankfully, as an introverted person, this is not as hard as you think. In fact, if you do this right, you will be tapping into your existing individual strengths. Put simply, effective problem solving is the ability to clearly define the problem, figure out its underlying nature, break it up into simple parts, and then try to plug in solutions to the parts that are problematic or challenging.

In other words, its structural nature is right up your alley. Make no mistake, solving problems in group settings is crucial to life's success, because a lot of times we find ourselves in a group. It's not like all our problems are individual in nature. A lot of the issues we face are group problems.

What complicates this is that oftentimes, people play hot potato with group problems. They think at the back of their heads that somebody else will take care of the problem. And guess what? The challenge gets bigger and bigger until it takes more resources and time than it otherwise would have if people solved it the first time around.

It's very important to learn how to solve problems in a group setting so you can communicate the solutions effectively with others. This helps trigger their own innate problem-solving skills and everybody benefits accordingly, because when you do this, you tap into your individual problem-solving competencies.

Again, the good news is introverts are hardwired to solve problems. The issue here is knowing enough to communicate the solutions effectively to others so the group, as a whole, benefits.

Step by step instructions for more effective group problem-solving

Step #1: Do your thing as an introvert

As an introvert, you know how to slice and dice any issue. You can break up any problem into its different parts and toss these parts backwards and forwards in your head. The key is to zero in; tightly define what the problem is.

Just because it makes sense in your head, doesn't mean that once you open your mouth it would make sense to people who hear you. You have to be clear, in plain English, about what the problem is. Also, look at specific perspective on the problem.

Is this the only approach to the problem, or are there other ways of looking at the problem? Consider the alternative views people may have about these issues.

Step #2 : List down the solutions that you think solves the problem

There is your solution, and then there's other people's solution. On a purely individual basis, you might be thinking that your personal solution is enough. I agree with you. It is enough, because you can solve the issue right there and then, but the challenge is this is a group problem.

So everybody has to buy in. Everybody has to feel that they are part of the process of solving this problem. If you were to just say to people that you just came back from the mountaintop and you have this ultimate solution in your arms, people are more likely to oppose you.

You're more likely to trigger to common refrain "Who do you think you are? Do you think you're better than me?" As you probably can imagine, this is not exactly good for interpersonal dynamics as well as working towards a common objective.

The better approach is to look at your solution, and then look at other potential solutions that other people could come up with. Don't pre-judge these. Look at their commonalities, and then present them as alternatives.

So instead of saying that there is one absolute, one-size-fits-all solution to this problem, namely yours, allow yourself to be perceived as open-minded. When you do this, you break down the problem, and then you present the different solutions with their advantages and disadvantages with no seeming preference for one answer over another.

Step #3 :Work with the group to decide on a solution

As offensive as it is for somebody to come up with "the answer," it is also off-putting to strong-arm everybody into picking your solution. When you work with others to solve a common problem, make it a group solution.

In other words, everybody has to have skin in the game. Everybody has to at least feel that they had some sort of input regarding the eventual decision. If you insist on just pushing your particular answer, then people will get the impression that you believe that it's your way or the highway. That's going to create or exacerbate existing divisions, and you probably will end up creating enemies, or making even worse enemies.

Decide on a solution in a group way, and clearly explain the pros and cons of each. This way, everybody feels that they were heard. Everybody feels that they had an equal space on the table.

Step #4 : Be part of the implementation

When presenting a solution to a group of people, make sure that everybody plays a part. Don't just say, "Okay, I have the answer, I'll do it myself." You have to be able to chop up the answer and allow people to take ownership. This not only makes your life easier, but it also makes the whole group problem-solution process more efficient.

You're splitting up resources and you're saving time, and you'll be more likely tapping into each other's core competencies. The quality of the solution that you are able to effect would be much better than if somebody just took the ball and ran with it.

Step #5 : Always do a post-mortem

It's always a good idea to look at the results and get everybody to buy in. Get everybody to pick apart the results so you can identify areas for improvement and do a better job. This is no time to become emotionally wedded to the solution that you submitted.

If it wasn't the best solution, or if there are areas for improvement, take it with a grain of salt. Roll with the punches and allow everybody to step in, and improve on what you contributed. Don't think that just because you came up with an idea, that when people try to change it, modify it, build it, or roll it back, that this is somehow an insult to you.

You're not improving your people skill that way. Remember, the whole focus of group problem solution is to work towards a common good.

Chapter 8: How Introverts Can Support and Motivate Others

It's easy to think that you already know how to encourage others. It's easy to believe that we know how to praise other people or provide some sort of positive feedback. But just like with a lot of introverts' communication patterns things are not as obvious to the other side of the conversation.

On our end, it may seem that we're communicating our praise, gratitude and appreciation loud and clear. However, you can't assume that the person you're directing your positive feedback to is receiving your feedback the way you intended.

It's not uncommon for introverts to try to praise somebody and it comes off as sarcastic, ironic, or, in one way or another, incomplete. In fact, a lot of times, introverts send a message that is perceived the complete opposite way by the intended recipient.

Has this ever happened to you? This produces a lot of awkward situations. Instead of cementing your social bonds and making your relationships stronger, you might actually end up poisoning your relationships.

The worst part to all of this is that you have all the best intentions in the world. You obviously didn't want to send the wrong message. In fact, you intended the opposite effect.

The problem is, the world doesn't care about your intentions. It couldn't care less about what motivates you. Instead, it focuses on what you actually did.

This is why you have to support and motivate others the right way.

How crucial is peer encouragement in any kind of group environment? Well, according to a study that came out in the journal Psychology in January 2011, people who receive encouragement from their peers tend to perform better than people who got encouragement from their superiors.

If you're working in any kind of group environment, this is a big deal.

How come? Well, when people feel properly motivated in your group, you are able to collectively accomplish common goals faster and more efficiently. You take up less resources. This can easily mean that everybody ends up happier.

Similarly, according to a Gallup study released in July 2004 in the business journal of the Gallup organization, 10,000 businesses were surveyed and this yielded feedback from over 4 million employees.

According to this comprehensive study, people who receive any kind of recognition or praise from their higher ups perform better than people who didn't.

What is the net impact of praise and institutional recognition? First of all, it increases individual employee productivity. It also boosts engagement among work group members.

This is a big deal because when people are more engaged with each other in a work environment, they are more likely to exchange solutions and bounce around ideas. This is the essence of Six Sigma training.

Six Sigma is a management philosophy that recognizes that a lot of innovations in organizations are actually pioneered from the grassroots. They don't come from top management and work their way down.

Real innovations that push the organization forward or take it to a whole other level come from individual workers doing their day to day tasks.

Unfortunately, a lot of these innovations stay with the individual worker. They never get around to sharing these hacks or tricks with coworkers, much less higher ups. While these productivity-boosting techniques can help them on an individual basis, it doesn't really benefit the organization as a whole.

Six Sigma is a system that encourages the percolation of individual level innovations and disruptions so it can benefit the whole enterprise.

Unfortunately, for Six Sigma to truly work, there has to be an environment of trust, openness and engagement.

When organizations regularly give praise and some token of recognition for rank and file team members, individual employees are more likely to engage with each other. This means that ideas are more likely to percolate up and feed into official Six Sigma corporate infrastructures.

Even if the organization hasn't heard of Six Sigma, the fact that people are exchanging ideas can lead to better overall group performance.

The Gallup study also found that when employees get positive feedback and recognition from the organizations that hired them, they, in turn, pay this forward.

How? Customers are more likely to feel the good morale of employees and are more likely to be satisfied with the services provided by the organization as a whole. This translates to higher levels of customer loyalty and increased levels of customer retention. This is phenomenal.

Please understand that the cheapest yet most effective source of new businesses are old customers. When you are engaging with old customers, they are more likely to buy from you because they've already experienced the value you bring to the table.

They are less likely to take a gamble with other brands or organizations they haven't done business with. As much as possible, they would rather order from you.

When your organization motivates rank and file employees to the point that they deliver better service, this process makes it easier for your existing customer base to stick with you.

Finally, according to the Gallup study, higher levels of employee recognition and praise translate to less job accidents and an improved overall safety record.

Make no mistake, people thrive on feedback. It's really important to communicate positive feedback with people around you so not only can you benefit on an individual level, but your team as a unit can live up to its fullest organizational potential.

Finally, in a study published in the journal Social and Personality Psychology Compass in August 2010 by a team out of the University of Chicago, researchers discovered that the type of feedback given to people have different effects.

When people are given positive feedback, they're more likely to commit to a goal. On the other hand, when individuals are given negative feedback, they become more motivated to try to improve things.

These are two totally different objectives. It's very important for management to know the difference and apply the right feedback mechanisms to produce their desired outcome.

Step by Step Instructions for Introverts Looking to Communicate Feedback the Right Way

Step #1: Commit to simple communication

When you're complimenting somebody, get straight to the point. That's the bottom line.

Avoid drawing it out. Avoid plugging in a lot of details. When you do that, you come off as flattering instead of leaving an actual insightful and honest assessment.

You have to understand that feedback, although it is very complimentary, is intended to communicate information.

When it increasingly looks like you're not really communicating and out to further some sort of agenda by flattering somebody, don't be surprised if you produce a negative effect. They think that you're just gossiping or you're just blowing smoke up their backside.

As you can well imagine, this is the opposite of your intended effect.

Accordingly, if you're going to compliment somebody and leave positive feedback, get straight to the point, keep it simple, and keep it realistic.

Step #2: Tell people positive things about them personally

When you are criticizing somebody, it's always a good idea to criticize what they did, not them personally. This way, there is a division between their output and their essence as human beings. They are less likely to take your feedback personally.

On the other hand, when you are complimenting somebody, make sure that it is personal. Make sure that you can relate it to some sort of trait they have.

Instead of simply saying, "I like the survey that you did," you focus instead on complimenting their imagination, insight and initiative which produced the survey.

See the difference? Focus on the process that is rooted to their personal characteristics instead of the actual work product

Step #3: Compliment people who deserve to be complimented

For this step, you have to overcome your ego.

It's very easy to compliment people that we like. It's very easy to feel positive about people we know will reciprocate the favor. It's hard to praise somebody who you know is working against you or is actively competing against you.

But if you want to develop a reputation for professionalism and you want your feedback to carry a lot more weight, you have to set your ego aside.

Call it for what it is. If you see somebody that you normally don't like do something that you like, let them know and let everybody else know.

If you keep this up, eventually, you will develop a reputation for being a straight shooter. This is the very best outcome that you should expect.

This way, when you compliment other people in the future, they know you're saying the truth. You're not being selective or playing political games.

Step #4: Encourage even the tiniest effort

It's very easy to just say that you're going to reward results and disregard effort. I can understand this because, let's face it, that's how the world judges you.

It couldn't care less about your feelings, and it definitely doesn't have time for your protests of how hard you tried. All it cares about is whether you achieved success or not.

Either you failed or you succeeded. Either you made it, or you fell short. The world is black and white.

However, if you are trying to improve your people skills as an introvert, you have to set this aside. Let the change begin with you. Instead of always zeroing in on people's results, focus on their effort.

Please understand that a lot of people try really hard, but, for whatever reason, they can't seem to get it together. Hey, it happens even to the very best of us.

So, when you stand out as the person who actually rewards effort by praising people, even if they made a very slight effort, you stand out from the crowd. This may be the spark of motivation they need to keep pushing forward to achieve greater and greater results.

On the other hand, if you're going to be a stickler for standards and insist only on results, don't be surprised if people quit. Don't be surprised if people think that the situation they're in is simply impossible and that they would probably be better off doing something else.

Step #5: Rehearse your demonstration of encouragement

As I have mentioned previously, it's very easy for introverts to think that they are already communicating their appreciation loud and clear.

After all, they're feeling it strongly deep down inside.

Well, the problem is, if you're not a very expressive person, you might send the wrong message. Your compliment might seem ironic or even downright sarcastic.

So, do yourself a big favor, try to make your encouragement as outward, objective, and as easy to understand as possible.

For example, if you say to somebody, "You did a great job hitting our sales target this quarter," instead of just patting that person on the back or giving that person a kind word in front of other people, hand that person some sort of plaque, a trophy, a gift, a gift certificate, or anything physical that screams out to the rest of the world "I'm not only complimenting this person with my mouth, I actually mean it because there's an actual physical manifestation of this encouragement."

It also helps if you look at your body language, your facial gestures, your tone of voice, and other nonverbal signals to make sure that they line up with the enthusiasm and warmth of the message you're trying to convey.

Chapter 9: How To Improve Your Flexibility and Open-Mindedness

How many times have you run across otherwise intelligent people who are so close-minded that they basically turn you off? I'm sure you've come across more than a couple of those people. In fact, these individuals are all too common.

It seems that the older we get, the more set in our ways we become. It's as if we reach a point where when we detect certain patterns or see certain stimuli, we automatically assume that we've seen it all and we automatically know how things will play out.

While this is kind of useful in many situations and adds a welcome level of efficiency as far as thinking is concerned, this way of thinking tends to push away people.

You basically are communicating to people that unless they talk a certain way or they have certain things that you expect, you can't be bothered.

This is a serious problem because if you have a closed mind, it's going to be very hard to learn. Just as it's very hard to learn if you constantly interrupt and talk over the person you're conversing with, it's hard to pick up on new ideas when your mind is closed.

Being open-minded simply means that you are open to new ideas. You haven't closed any possibilities. You haven't dismissed any opportunities out of hand.

Also, being open-minded means that despite your own views, you are open to entertaining other people's views. And more importantly, recognizing the value of those views.

Please understand that it's hard to communicate on a person to person basis if the other person can tell you're going to reject their opinion or knowledge out of hand.

As you probably already know, people are very possessive of their intellectual output. It's one thing to say, "I'm not criticizing you personally. I'm criticizing your opinion," but it's another to actually be on the receiving end of that.

Because if people oppose your opinion, it's not that hard to assume that they're opposing you. It becomes personal. At some level or another, it becomes emotional, and this creates an artificial boundary between you and that other person.

Instead of working towards a common goal, sharing vital new ideas, and otherwise increasing each other's value, it becomes adversarial and, worse yet, mutually exclusive. So, a little bit of open-mindedness can go a long way when it comes to people skills.

Be open to people without necessarily being a patsy, a dupe, or a gullible person. Just because you're willing to consider what other people have to say, it doesn't automatically mean that you're going to jump in with both feet and take whatever they're dishing out hook, line and sinker. That's another matter entirely.

You're not losing your dignity by being open-minded. You're not being simple-minded or stupid. Instead of looking at this with a tremendous sense of insecurity or a sense of vulnerability, understand that being open is a crucial part of being a living, thriving, thinking human being.

Open-mindedness, whether you like it or not, can improve the quality of your life. You'd be surprised as to how well other people's ideas can improve your life.

Maybe they can open doors of opportunity, maybe they can help you think about how you normally do things and this can improve many things in your life. There are just so many ways you can benefit from other people.

But if you think that you have to preemptively shut them out because you're threatened by their ideas or you think you already have them figured out, the only person that's suffering is you.

They're not suffering because they have something to offer. Eventually, they'll get in touch with others who are more receptive and both of them can benefit. You end up losing out.

Being open-minded can actually benefit you physically. In fact, according to a 2012 study published in the Journal of Aging and Health, a higher level of personal openness can lead to a longer life.

In a massive study of 1,349 men, people who have a sense of openness have higher survival rates over an 18-year mortality period. When people are open-minded, they are more creative. This leads to lower mortality risks.

Please understand that the openness that this study isolates as leading to a longer life has to do with creativity. The good news is, you can be a creative person without necessarily being an artist, a poet or a writer.

You can be a creative person by being a sales person. You just have to have the right creative attitude regardless of your line of work.

When you are always looking at different ways of doing things or achieving certain outcomes, you are being open-minded and creative, and this can actually lengthen your life.

Open-Mindedness Leads to Flexibility

If you're feeling stuck or you feel that your relationships are often trapped in certain fixed patterns, it may be because you're just being inflexible. In other words, you'll have stop embracing novelty.

When you learn how to embrace the new, and I'm talking about new experiences, new places and new people, you start looking at everything you have from a new perspective and things are possible again. It's harder for you to feel stuck. It's harder for you to feel that your best years are behind you.

In a 2017 study published in the Journal of Research in Personality, University of Melbourne researchers worked with 134 test participants to test their eyesight and see if their openness to pressing certain buttons enable them to perceive more stimuli.

The study confirmed that people are more likely to perceive new combinations when they are open-minded. This means that when it comes to your creativity, you are more likely to come up with new combinations or new solutions if you are flexible and open-minded.

Similarly, in a 2009 study published in the Journal of Personality and Social Psychology, 205 MBA students were surveyed and their travel habits were correlated to their survey responses. It turns out that people who travel more frequently are more open to new experiences and this can have a profound impact on their mindset.

Step by Step Instructions for Increasing Your Mental Flexibility

Step #1: Identify your intellectual blind spots

Every person has a list of favored and disfavored intellectual topics. For most people, these favored topics involve disciplines like science or math.

As you can well imagine, these fields have many different levels and have many different areas. Some are more fun and accessible than others.

If your blind spot is math, look for fun math problems or interesting and quirky math studies to read. You just might end up surprising yourself. It may well turn out that you might find these things interesting, or at least more interesting than you had originally thought. Keep pushing yourself in this direction.

Everybody's got intellectual blind spots. Keep exploring all these blind spots and dig even deeper.

For example, you may start out with fun math and logic exercises. Once you've gotten used to those, take on more dry and academic material.

Before you know it, you will become very comfortable with these bodies of knowledge instead of doing what you normally do, which is to dismiss them out of hand or fear them.

Step #2: Travel as much as possible

Don't get me wrong. I understand that most people do not have the budget to travel extensively. But did you know, in your city or state or province, there are lots of places you haven't been to before?

When I was living in California, I didn't even check out a lot of the museums and national parks and other travel attractions there.

You don't have to get on a plane to go halfway around the world to "travel." You can travel where you are.

Make sure you fully explore your neighborhood. Maybe start by walking around the block and paying attention to small details.

Once you've done that, expand by checking out larger sets of blocks in your area. Take a look at local attractions, familiarize yourself with local landmarks – there are so many ways you can do this.

And the best part? You don't need a budget. You're already doing this.

You're already going from Point A to Point B. But instead of just focusing on getting to work, why not pay attention to all the scenery that you otherwise fail to notice getting to work. Do you see where I'm coming from?

The best part is that once you get used to this, it becomes a lot of fun. You start looking at exploring your surroundings with a sense of adventure, discover and curiosity. This makes you a more inquisitive and open-minded person.

Step #3: Challenge yourself by getting out of your comfort zone

A lot of people are creatures of comfort. We like to hang out with the same people, we like to read the same stuff, we like to watch the same type of entertainment and do the same types of activities. We feel that it gives us a sense of control.

We definitely appreciate the routine nature of our day-to-day lives because things aren't popping off all over the place. There's no chaos, and we feel that this is a good thing.

The problem is, the more you stay within the safe confines of your comfort zone, the more the walls of your comfort zone start to cave in around you. They start to limit you. They start to freeze you from the great experiences you could otherwise be enjoying.

Worst of all, they freeze or calcify your mindset to the extent that you don't want to challenge the familiar, the routine, and the comfortable and convenient. You feel that you're entitled to things being quick, familiar and easy.

And unfortunately, life doesn't work that way. Oftentimes, life throws you a curve ball and it ends up knocking you off track.

So, to head this off, push against your comfort zone. Do things that aren't all that normal. Explore things that aren't all that comfortable for you. For example, if the idea of speaking in public scares the stuffing out of you, do that.

It doesn't have to be big. For example, if you don't like talking to strangers, start talking to coffee shop baristas.

The great thing about that is that they have no choice. They are paid to talk with you. They're not paid to brush you off, they can't be rude to you, so you're dealing with a captive audience, and you can pretty much experiment and push your personal limits.

The best part to all of this is that it doesn't have to be big. You don't have to be some sort of hero. You don't have to overdo it. Even just moving out of your comfort zone a few inches every single day is more than enough.

Step #4: Consciously seek to learn from others

If you are struggling in any area of your life, don't think that other people don't already have the answer. You know the answer to this.

Whatever issue you're struggling with, somebody has already mastered. Somebody already knows the answer. They already have the key. The challenge is to find those people and listening to them.

Make no mistake, you can learn from other people. This is why it's really important to try to learn from as many different people as possible.

Even if they don't have technical solutions to the specific challenges you're facing, you can at least choose to be inspired by them.

Everybody goes through ups and downs. Everybody gets knocked down by challenges from time to time. Get inspired by these people.

Ask for their story. Ask for how they solved their problem. And, at the very least, allow yourself to be inspired by the fact that they got back up after they got knocked down. After all, if they can do it, you can do it too.

Step #5: Be honest with yourself

The main reason why people become close-minded is because they think they have everything figured out. They think that they know things well enough and that trying to explore new things is more bother than it's worth.

The problem is, a lot of this is tied to ego. The truth is, you're not all-knowing. Not by a long shot.

Nobody is perfect. Nobody knows all the answers. This is why it's a good idea to just be completely honest with yourself and know that you don't know.

By being completely honest, you're not actually making yourself vulnerable or weak. You're not losing any dignity or pride. Instead, you're making yourself stronger because the only thing we know is the fact that we don't know everything.

Once you understand that fundamental truth, then everything starts becoming possible again. You become open to learning from people who might have the information you need to get to the next level.

Compare this with thinking that you know everything and your conclusion is that it's impossible. If that's your mindset, then you're stuck.

It's hard to achieve any kind of progress because you've closed off any possibility of solutions.

There are no solutions. You're stuck. It's like you're in a pit both mentally and physically.

By simply owning up to the incompleteness of your knowledge, you're not losing anything. If anything, you're just like everybody else. Everybody else is clueless at some level or another. Welcome to the club.

So, do yourself a big favor, be completely honest regarding your limitations. A little bit of honesty goes a long way.

Chapter 10: Develop a Sense of Humor for Better Interpersonal Relations

I don't know about you, but the world can be a crazy place. It's very chaotic. A lot of your best laid plans simply fail to pan out. That's just the way reality works.

The sad situation is that I notice too many people expect the world to be perfect. They expect things to happen on cue. In fact, in many cases, they rob themselves of the happiness they could otherwise be enjoying by insisting on things to be perfect.

I don't know about you, but the world isn't perfect. It never was. And I suspect it never will be.

You just have to take it for what it is. It is what it is. This is why having a sense of humor is really important, especially when it comes to person to person skills.

If you are able to laugh at your situation and laugh at yourself, people are more likely to like you. People are more likely to think that you are approachable and they can deal with you.

The worst thing that people have to deal with is somebody who takes themselves so seriously that everything is a chore or everything is some sort of challenge.

Let me tell you, if that's your attitude, you bring out the worst in people. It's as if they are basically walking on eggshells around you.

They probably would gladly oblige you for quite some time, but eventually, it will get old. Eventually, people will become impatient and they will push back.

They'll say to you, "Why am I denying myself when I'm around you? I'm just going to let it all hang out. Forget these rules."

That's exactly the kind of blowback you don't want or need. A little bit of humor can go a long way.

When you have a great sense of humor, you see the absurdity in everything that happens in life. Because hey, let's be honest, at some level or another, life is absurd. It's full of ironies. It's full of dashed hopes, missed expectations, and tragedies.

At some level or another, you just have to sit back and laugh it off. That's how you get rid of the tension and the worry.

Compare this with basically sucking it all in and expecting everything to be perfect, and then coming apart when things don't pan out. I think the choice is obvious.

Just How Crucial is Humor in Personal Interactions?

Well, according to the Journal of Neuroscience, when we laugh, our brains actually produce endorphins. These are chemicals that have a similar structure to opioids like heroin and opium.

In other words, when you laugh sincerely and honestly, you are releasing all-natural drugs in your system that reduces tension and gives you a sense of euphoria, ease and relaxation.

It's an all-natural legal way to get "high." And all you have do is laugh with other people.

Also, when you laugh, it socially lubricates your situation. You no longer have to feel like you're going out on a limb to share something. You can easily pass it off by laughing both at yourself or at the situation. In this sense, laughter and humor are great for strengthening social bonds.

Step by Step Directions for Improving Your Social Sense of Humor

Don't think for a second that either you're born with a sense of humor or you're not. Please understand that the best comedians and stand-up comics weren't made. A lot of them developed their impeccable sense of timing through observation and training.

In fact, even the funniest comedians like Louis CK started out bombing. Joke after joke, all they can got were crickets. But now, they're some of the most highly paid comedians on the planet because they kill the crowd each and every time.

You can do the same. I'm not saying that you're going to be the next Louis CK, but I'm saying that the way you tell jokes and your sense of humor can be improved. It may not seem like it, but with enough time, focus and commitment, you can.

Here are the steps that you can take to improve your sense of humor.

Step #1: Expose yourself to funny stuff

The great thing about the internet is that you're only a click away from great comedy. There are tons of amazingly funny comedy videos on YouTube. Expose yourself to these people.

Please understand that comedy is all about timing. Somebody can say something that is borderline funny and kill the crowd because of their timing.

On the other hand, somebody can say something that is genuinely laugh out loud funny, but their delivery is so deadpan and so awkward that the best reaction it could get are crickets. See the difference?

A lot of it has to do with delivery instead of content. But the only way you can see the difference is when you constantly expose yourself to this material. Otherwise, you wouldn't know which is which.

Step #2: Share a joke with your friends and family more regularly

Let's face it, everybody's shared a joke at least once. You hear a funny joke and you think it's the funniest thing since sliced bread, so you say it to your brother or sister. They don't think it's funny or they look at you weird. That's pretty much the extent of your experience cracking jokes.

Well, what if I told you that if you just keep it up and you just kept telling jokes on a fairly consistent basis, you'll get better at it?

Remember, it's all about timing. It's all about set up, and it's all about delivery. But unfortunately, you're probably not going to get better at it if you don't try it regularly enough.

Practice makes perfect. The more you do something, the better you get at it. So, get into the habit of sharing as many different jokes as you can with friends and family members.

At first, it's going to be awkward. Sometimes they would be very discouraging. But if you keep at it, eventually, you will get them to laugh.

Step #3: Focus on timing and knowing your audience

I wish I could tell you that comedic giants like Richard Pryor, Robin Williams, Louis CK and David Chappelle kill crowds across the board and at all times. Well, unfortunately, that's not true.

The reason why George Carlin and other classic giants of comedy are so effective and devastating is because they know their audience and they know how to time a joke properly. You can do the same.

You know who your friends are. You know the preferences of your family members. Armed with this information, you can then time your jokes better. You can position your jokes better, and this can increase the chances of you getting the intended effect.

Just because your joke bombed the first hundred times, it doesn't mean that you have to stop trying. All this failure tells you is that you need to pay closer attention to your audience so you can eventually achieve success.

Step #4: Learn to laugh at yourself

This is the foundation of effective comedy. People who don't know how to laugh at themselves make for lousy comics.

If you don't take yourself seriously and you're just looking to have a good time with people, there is a good chance that a lot of that improvisational spirit and candidness will show through and people would have a good time.

Remember, people are not going to be comfortable around you if they can tell you're uncomfortable about yourself. So the more comfortable you are with yourself, the more people will laugh at your jokes.

This is why you need to learn to laugh at yourself first. Stop taking yourself seriously.

Please understand that the universe doesn't revolve around you. So what, you get insulted? So what, you feel offended by certain topics? Life goes on.

The more you laugh at yourself and the thicker your skin gets, the better it will be for you as far as your jokes go.

Conclusion

Introverts are generally misunderstood people. Introverts actually have social skills. Introverts are actually fond of having people around. The big challenge is that when you're an introvert, it takes a lot more energy for you to communicate socially with others.

Unlike extroverts who draw their energy from other people, introverts' energy levels are drained by prolonged social contact. This is why it's really important to understand the people skills described in this book and position them and practice them in such a way that they give you the energy and motivation you need to keep stepping up your game.

Don't expect things to become perfect overnight. You just have to keep trying.

And also, don't expect overnight success and encouragement. What's important is that you properly stimulate yourself with the right people, with the right influences, so you eventually will be able to produce the outcome that you desire from yourself.

I wish you nothing but the greatest success.

completeness of the contents of this work and specifically disclaims all warranties, including without limitation warranties of fitness for a particular purpose. No warranty may be created or extended by sales or promotional materials. The advice and recipes contained herein may not be suitable for everyone. This work is sold with the understanding that the author is not engaged in rendering medical, legal or other professional advice or services. If professional assistance is required, the services of a competent professional person should be sought. The author shall not be liable for damages arising here from. The fact that an individual, organization of website is referred to in this work as a citation and/or potential source of further information does not mean that the author endorses the information the individual, organization to website may provide or recommendations they/it may make. Further, readers should be aware that Internet websites listed in this work might have changed or disappeared between when this work was written and when it is read.

Adherence to all applicable laws and regulations, including international, federal, state, and local governing professional licensing, business practices, advertising, and all other aspects of doing business in any jurisdiction in the world is the sole responsibility of the purchaser or reader.

www.ingramcontent.com/pod-product-compliance
Lightning Source LLC
Chambersburg PA
CBHW022018170526
45157CB00003B/1273